Transporte público
Public Transportation

¡VAMOS A TOMAR
EL TREN!

LET'S TAKE THE
TRAIN!

Elisa Peters

Traducido por Eida de la Vega

PowerKiDS
press.

New York

For my father, who has always loved trains, and Akarawint Blitstein, a young train enthusiast

Published in 2015 by The Rosen Publishing Group, Inc.
29 East 21st Street, New York, NY 10010

First Edition

Spanish translation: Eida de la Vega

Editor: Amelie von Zumbusch
Photo Research: Katie Stryker
Book Design: Andrew Povolny

Photo Credits:Cover christian Lagereek/iStock/Thinkstock; p. 5 BestPhotoPlus/Shutterstock.com; p. 6 James Devaney/Contributor/WireImage/Getty Images; p. 9 auremar/Shutterstock.com; p. 10 Jorg Hackemann/ Shutterstock.com; p. 13 Claver Carroll/PhotoLibrary/Getty Images; p. 14 Yenwen Lu/E+/Getty Images; p. 17 Bloomberg/Contributor/Getty Images; p. 18 Superstock/Getty Images; p. 21 Jiawangkun/Shutterstock.com; p. 22 Bíró Gabriella/iStock/Thinkstock.

Publisher's Cataloging Data

Peters, Elisa.
Let's take the train! = ¡Vamos a tomar el tren! / by Elisa Peters ; translated by Eida de la Vega. — 1st ed. — New York : PowerKids Press, c2015
          p. cm. — (Public transportation = Transporte público)
English and Spanish.
Includes an index.
ISBN: 978-1-4777-6781-8 (Library Binding)
1. Railroad trains—Juvenile literature. 2. Railroad travel—Juvenile literature.   I. Vega, Eida de la, translator. II. Title.
III. Title: ¡Vamos a tomar el tren!
TF148.P48 2015
385

Websites: Due to the changing nature of Internet links, PowerKids Press has developed an online list of websites related to the subject of this book. This site is updated regularly. Please use this link to access the list: www.powerkidslinks.com/putr/train/

Manufactured in the United States of America

CPSIA Compliance Information: Batch #WS14PK4: For Further Information contact Rosen Publishing, New York, New York at 1-800-237-9932

Contenido

Contents

Es divertido viajar en tren.
Te subes en la estación.

It is fun to take the train. You
get on at the station.

Busca un asiento.
El conductor te pedirá
el boleto.

Find a seat. The conductor will
take your ticket.

El maquinista maneja el tren.
¡Los trenes pueden ir rápido!

The engineer drives the train.
Trains can go fast!

Cada tren tiene varios vagones. El vagón que tira del tren es la **locomotora**.

Each train has several cars. The car that pulls the train is the **locomotive**.

Los trenes corren sobre **raíles** de acero. Los raíles se apoyan en **traviesas**. Las traviesas son de madera o de concreto.

Trains run on steel **tracks**. The tracks sit on **ties**. Ties are made of wood or concrete.

Los trenes de pasajeros transportan personas.
Los trenes de carga transportan mercancías.

Passenger trains carry people.
Freight trains carry goods.

Los trenes Amtrak corren entre ciudades de los Estados Unidos. Los más rápidos son los Acela.

Amtrak trains run between US cities. The fastest Amtrak trains are Acela trains.

El primer ferrocarril de los Estados Unidos fue el *B&O Railroad*. "B&O" quiere decir "Baltimore y Ohio".

The first railroad in the United States was the B&O Railroad. "B&O" is short for "Baltimore and Ohio."

En el Sitio Histórico Nacional Steamtown hay un montón de trenes antiguos.
Es un museo del tren en Scranton, Pensilvania.

Steamtown National Historic Site has a lot of old trains.
It is a train museum in Scranton, Pennsylvania.

¿Conoces a alguien que haya viajado en tren?

Has anyone you know taken a train?

PALABRAS QUE DEBES SABER / WORDS TO KNOW

(la) locomotora

locomotive

(la) traviesa

tie

(el) raíl

track

ÍNDICE

INDEX